DANGEROUS DRUGS

RITALIN AND ADDERALL

JACKIE F. STANMYRE

Cavendish
Square

New York

Library of Congress Cataloging-in-Publication Data

Stanmyre, Jackie.
Ritalin and adderall / Jackie Stanmyre.
pages cm. — (Dangerous drugs)
Includes glossary.
Includes bibliographical references and index.
ISBN 978-1-50260-554-2 (hardcover) ISBN 978-1-50260-555-9 (ebook)
1. Medication abuse. 2. Teenagers—Drug use. 3. Methylphenidate—Side effects. I. Title.

RM146.S73 2015
362.29—dc23

2014049268

Editorial Director: David McNamara
Editor: Fletcher Doyle
Copy Editor: Rebecca Rohan
Art Director: Jeffrey Talbot
Designer: Stephanie Flecha
Senior Production Manager: Jennifer Ryder-Talbot
Production Editor: Renni Johnson
Photo Research: J8 Media

The photographs in this book are used by permission and through the courtesy of: Chris Gallagher/Getty Images, cover; Jamie Grill/Getty Images, 4; Colleen Cahill/Age Fotostock, 7; Patrick Mallahan III, File:Adderall XR 20mg.jpg/Wikimedia Commons, 10; Sponge, File:Ritalin-SR-20mg-full.jpg/Wikimedia Commons, 11; Otto Greule Jr/Getty Images, 12; Ute Grabowsky/Photothek via Getty Images, 16; Public Domain, File:Dopamine 3D ball.png/Wikimedia Commons, 18; Age Fotostock/Getty Images, 22; Wavebreakmedia/Shutterstock, 23; Catherine Yeulet/Thinkstock, 25; Moment/Getty Images, 28; Vetta/Getty Images, 33; Madhourse/Thinkstock, 35; Pedrosala/Shutterstock, 37; David McNew/Getty Images, 38; Alexander Trinitatov/Shutterstock, 41; Sturti/iStock, 44-45; Neustockimages/iStock, 47; Shane Hansen/iStock, 49; Digitalskillet/iStock, 51; LeoPatrizi/iStock, 55; KatarzynaBialasiewicz/Thinkstock, 57.

Printed in the United States of America

Contents

CHAPTER ONE

The Wrong Solution

IT'S LATE AT NIGHT AND THERE'S A BIG chemistry exam tomorrow. A few more hours of studying are needed for you to feel confident in passing the test, but you can barely keep your eyes open.

You're invited to a friend's party, but you don't know a lot of people who will be there—so you're feeling a little shy. For once, instead of being a wallflower, you want to feel more energetic and talkative. You want to stay up all night. How can you make this happen?

Far too often, students rely on **stimulant** drugs, such as Ritalin or Adderall, to help them stay alert, awake, and focused. Sounds like the perfect solution, right? Wrong. When taken without a doctor's prescription, stimulants can lead to milder

Students who are having trouble concentrating on schoolwork may find themselves searching for any option—even illegal ones—to get the work done.

side effects such as nervousness and trouble sleeping, or those that are more severe such as visual **hallucinations** or violent behavior. Several cases of youths committing suicide due to Ritalin abuse have been reported.

Hallucinations are sensations that primarily cause a person to see or hear things that do not exist. The most common hallucination experienced by youth who take Ritalin is the feeling of being surrounded by insects, snakes, or worms. Some have reported feeling as if there are bugs crawling under their skin. People who have abused Adderall can experience **paranoia**—an overwhelming feeling that someone is "out to get them." One participant in a forum about Adderall **addiction** reported hiding in her house with a knife because she was convinced there was a gang outside trying to kill her. No one was actually there.

Drugs Called Other Names

Young people need to be on the lookout for these drugs because substances containing them won't always be called by their proper names. Other names for Ritalin include Kiddie Cocaine (or Kiddie Coke), Skittles, Vitamin R, Smarties, Poor Man's Cocaine, Diet Coke, Rids, and R-ball. The nicknames often refer to cocaine because both Ritalin and cocaine fall into the same category of drugs, known as stimulants or "uppers." Street names for Adderall include Beans, Christmas Trees, Double Trouble, Pep Pills, Beanies, Dexies, Speed, and Black Beauties.

Adderall abuse can lead to paranoia, an unfounded fear someone is out to get you.

Ritalin and Adderall are often prescribed to young people with **Attention Deficit Hyperactivity Disorder**, or ADHD. These young people can have significant difficulty paying attention, sitting still, waiting their turn, or concentrating for extended periods of time. Most experts have determined ADHD is the result of abnormal chemical levels in the brain that impair a person's impulse control and ability to pay attention. In these cases, Ritalin and Adderall are used as medication to help students perform more effectively at school and at home.

These pills are ending up in the wrong hands—and with detrimental outcomes. Ritalin is one of the top ten stolen prescription drugs in the country. Between 1.6 and 3.4 percent of students in grades eight through twelve reported abusing Ritalin in the past year. And Ritalin use is part of a bigger problem, as high school students are using more and more prescription drugs without a doctor's prescription. The National Youth Risk Behavior Survey of 2013 asked students across the country if they had ever used these prescription drugs illegally. Saying "yes" were 12.4 percent of ninth graders, 17.3 percent of tenth graders, 20.8 percent of eleventh graders, and 21.3 percent of twelfth graders. States with the highest percentages were Alabama, Arkansas, Illinois, Louisiana, Nevada, Oklahoma, Tennessee, Texas, and Wyoming.

Other studies have shown that many who abuse prescription pills do not stop there. The National Survey on Drug Use and Health found people who used Adderall without a prescription were more likely to experiment with other illicit drugs. People who used Adderall not prescribed to them were more likely to have also used marijuana, cocaine, hallucinogens, inhalants, narcotic pain relievers, tranquilizers, methamphetamines, and sedatives than people who did not abuse Adderall in the past year. The largest overlap was found with marijuana users.

Despite the fact that hard drugs such as heroin are available, the Drug Enforcement Agency (DEA) still has Ritalin and Adderall on its radar. Ritalin and Adderall are classified as Schedule II Narcotics by the DEA. This means three things: (1) these drugs have a high potential for abuse,

(2) each is accepted for medical use in the United States, and (3) abuse of either can lead to severe psychological or physical dependence.

Psychological and physical dependence means one thing: addiction.

Made in a Lab

Ritalin and Adderall are considered stimulants, which is a class of drugs that stimulates the central nervous system, including the brain. Ritalin is made of **methylphenidate**, and Adderall is made of **amphetamines**. They function in the same way and have similar side effects.

The drug class of amphetamines was first synthesized by chemist Lazar Edeleano in 1887. Because amphetamines are synthetic drugs, they must be created in a lab, and they do not occur naturally. In addition to Adderall and Ritalin, other drugs in the stimulant class include Concerta, Dexedrine, DexoStrat, and Desoxyn.

Amphetamines were first used as a stimulant in the early 1930s. They were marketed as an inhaler for nasal congestion, and for treating asthma and other respiratory conditions. The range of ailments for which amphetamines were prescribed grew quickly to include alcohol hangover, narcolepsy, **depression**, weight reduction, and vomiting associated with pregnancy. During World War II, mostly in the early 1940s, the military in the United States, Great Britain, Germany, and Japan used amphetamines to improve mood and increase alertness and endurance. It was also

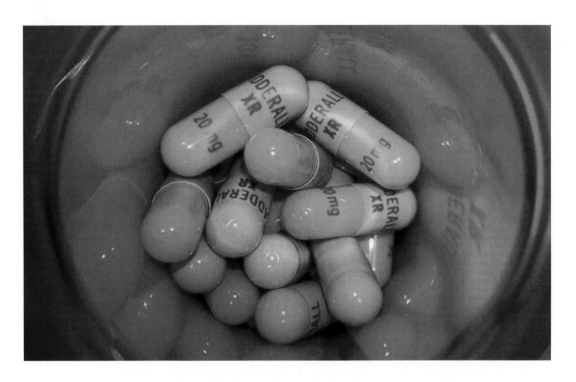

around this time that hyperactivity in young people was first treated with amphetamines.

The increase in medical use of amphetamines was due to their low price, availability, lasting effects, and because medical professionals did not they think were addictive.

Use Grows Rapidly

Ritalin was synthesized in 1944 by Leandro Panizzon and known by its generic name of methylphenidate, or MPH. The name "Ritalin" came from the first name of Panizzon's wife, Marguerite, who was known as "Rita." The formula was improved around 1950, and by 1954 tests on humans

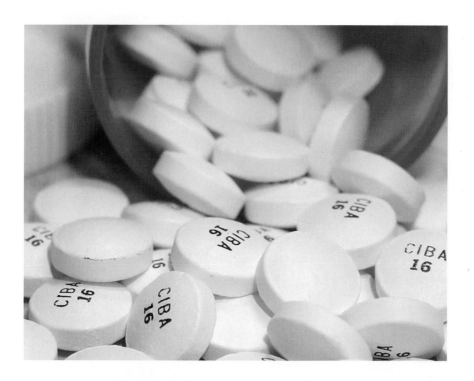

Ritalin and Adderall (previous page) may look as harmless as any other prescription drug from the doctor, but their use can be deadly.

commenced. In the 1950s and 1960s, medical professionals grew interested in using Ritalin to treat what was originally called "hyperkinetic syndrome," which later became known as Attention Deficit Hyperactivity Disorder. Doctors prescribing Ritalin for treatment purposes increased in the 1970s and early 1980s. Soon its use exploded in the United States. Between 1991 and 1999, Ritalin sales in the United States increased 500 percent.

Davis Strikes Out

The grips of illegal drug use can capture anyone. Chris Davis, a professional baseball player for the Baltimore Orioles, found that out the hard way. In September 2014, Davis was suspended for twenty-five games for failing a drug screen by testing positive for amphetamines. Davis admitted to using Adderall. It was the second time he had failed a drug test. He missed the end of the regular season and the playoffs.

"I apologize to my teammates, coaches, the Orioles organization and especially the fans," Davis said. "I made a mistake by taking Adderall."

Major League Baseball (MLB) offers therapeutic use exemptions to players with an illness or condition, allowing them to take necessary medication. Davis had an exemption to use Adderall during his three seasons with the Texas Rangers. However, baseball's owners and players decided to tighten the requirements for getting an

Baltimore Oriole Chris Davis was sent to the sidelines when he used Adderall without permission.

exemption in 2011 after requests for them increased. Davis was not allowed to renew the exemption after he was traded to Baltimore in 2012. A team of specialists could not find medical reasons for him to use the drug. That made his use illegal under MLB's rules even if he had a prescription. Davis received an exemption for 2015.

Stimulant use among baseball players has been on the rise, and the reported need for Adderall has skyrocketed. In 2006, MLB granted twenty-eight players the medical exemption allowing them to take Adderall. In 2013, 119 players were allowed to take the prescribed stimulant. That is nearly 10 percent of the players on all of baseball's forty-man Major League rosters combined.

The demand for Adderall has seen a similar increase in numbers. Because amphetamine drugs have such dangerous qualities, the DEA allows only a certain amount to be commercially manufactured each year. Congress votes annually on increasing the quota to help meet the rising demand for the drugs. In 1990, the United States was cleared to manufacture 417 kilograms (919 pounds) of amphetamine. In 2000, the number grew to 9,007 kilograms (19,857 pounds). By 2012, the number multiplied to 25,300 kilograms (55,777 pounds). Quick math will show that the United States increased the amount of amphetamines it made more than sixty-fold in a span of just twenty-two years.

The United States has become the international home base for these stimulants. In 2009, the United Nations' International Narcotics Board reported that despite being home to only 4 percent of the world's population, the United States produces 88 percent of the world's legal Ritalin type drugs. And Americans take an awful lot more of these drugs than everyone else, too. Per capita, Canadians use one-third the prescription stimulants of people in the United States, while Germans use one-eighth, Britons use one-twelfth, and Japanese one-fiftieth.

The National Drug Intelligence Center found the increase in prescriptions has increased the opportunity for abuse. The DEA has found adolescents who are prescribed Ritalin may give it or sell it to their classmates. Students want it because the drug can create feelings of euphoria, or extreme happiness. People began crushing the tablets into a powder and snorting it, or dissolving it into water to use as an injection into a vein. These **routes of administration** quicken the onset of the stimulating effects, compared to when the pills are taken by mouth. This means a person would get the "high" or alert feeling more quickly.

The United States has lagged behind other countries in recognizing the dangers of Ritalin abuse. Very early reports in Sweden led the country to remove Ritalin from its list of legal drugs in 1968. Recent attempts to crack down on

the drug's abuse potential have been defeated in the United States. In September 2014, a US doctor petitioned the Food and Drug Administration (FDA), stating that stimulants such as Adderall and Ritalin should be reformulated so they could not be crushed into a powder for snorting or injecting. The FDA rejected the petition because no one knew if the changes would alter the way the new drug worked. So for now, it's up to individuals taking the drugs to recognize the dangers of abusing them.

CHAPTER TWO

Calming Before the Storm

RITALIN, ADDERALL, AND THE ENTIRE stimulant drug family were a huge mystery to scientists until very recently.

As you have read, Ritalin's common name is methylphenidate. Other drugs that contain methylphenidate include Metadate, Methylin, and Concerta. Adderall contains a combination of the stimulants amphetamine and dextroamphetamine. Both types of drugs work to stimulate the central nervous system, which consists of the brain and spinal cord. Our central nervous system is in charge of sending messages throughout our body via **neurons**. When the nervous system is stimulated by drugs, mental

Ritalin and Adderall are both stimulants, but they can be used to calm hyperactivity.

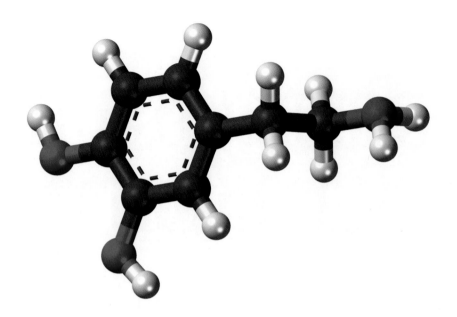

Dopamine is a chemical in our brains that helps regulate movement and emotion.

or physical functions may improve for a period of time, increasing alertness, attention, or energy.

Originally, medical professionals thought stimulants had **paradoxical** effects on individuals with ADHD—meaning they didn't affect the brain as one would expect. Stimulants increase alertness and activity. They speed up the body by raising heart rate and blood pressure. But for some reason they work to calm young people with ADHD, to help them focus and think more clearly. Scientists were stumped.

Finally, in the early 2000s, Dr. Nora Volkow headed a team that identified the reason Ritalin works so well for

young people for whom the drug has been appropriately prescribed and who take only the recommended **doses**. Dr. Volkow discovered that the brain of young adults with ADHD has too little of the incredibly valuable chemical **dopamine**.

"Dopamine is not only involved with movement and attention but with reward and motivation," Dr. Volkow reported. "It modulates brain signals that say, 'This is important! Pay attention!'" Dr. Volkow further explained that even when we are concentrating on a single task, other parts of our brain are working, too. In a child with ADHD, the other parts of their brain are working too hard, distracting the child from the task at hand. Ritalin works to increase dopamine to more normal levels. This helps the child focus on the main task and drowns out the distractions. This is the main benefit of Ritalin or Adderall for those who truly need it. The drugs allow them to calm their minds and bodies enough to sit still and pay attention.

Drugs Affect the Body

Whether taken appropriately or not, these drugs affect the body in other ways. Stimulants also increase blood pressure and heart rate, constrict blood vessels, increase blood glucose (the levels of sugar in the blood), and open breathing passages. For these reasons, it remains important for young people prescribed these medications to stay in touch with their doctors regarding potential side effects they may be experiencing. The dangers of these side effects also increase for those who use the drugs without a prescription and without a doctor's care.

Determining who really needs those medications has been an ongoing, controversial discussion. The Center for Disease Control's National Center on Birth Defects and Developmental Disabilities funded a study in 2012 to give us a better understanding of ADHD and its treatment. Researchers visited two diverse communities in South Carolina and Oklahoma and found that approximately 10 percent of young people between the ages of five and thirteen met the criteria for a diagnosis of ADHD. But, of those taking medications, such as Ritalin or Adderall, only 28 to 40 percent met the criteria for a diagnosis. This indicates doctors may be prescribing ADHD medications for young people who do not need them. For this reason, treatment alternatives are being explored, particularly for those youths who have mild symptoms but may not need to take a drug to manage them.

As young people have grown more informed about ADHD, more of them are lying about symptoms they experience to get the drug. This was the case with Richard Fee, a twenty-four-year-old college graduate who grew dangerously addicted to Adderall—even though he was under the care of a physician and held a prescription for the drugs, according to the *New York Times*. Fee spent a week in a psychiatric hospital after becoming violently delusional and still received another ninety-day prescription from his doctor. Two weeks later, he hanged himself in his

Doctors may appropriately prescribe Ritalin or Adderall for some children, but it still is important to know the risks.

bedroom closet. Fee's friends and family told the *New York Times* they watched him lie to doctors for years, faking his symptoms in order to make sure he could maintain his supply. A study published in the journal *Psychological Assessment* found that college students pretending to have ADHD symptoms were able to "pass" the test and fool doctors into thinking they had the disorder.

Many students have been known to turn to Adderall for binge studying or cramming sessions. One pill can provide a jolt of focus, energy, and purpose that students think is useful if they need six hours to finish a paper or eight hours to study flashcards for a test. Unfortunately, these students are overlooking the side effects of taking an unprescribed medication. This causes more harm than good to the human body.

PRESCRIBE RECESS

There are advantages of taking medications for some young adults diagnosed with Attention Deficit Hyperactivity Disorder, but researchers are starting to consider other, potentially safer options. A study published in September 2014 found that a twelve-week exercise program improved math and reading scores for all youth, but had an especially positive impact on those with signs of ADHD. And the previous year a similar study found just twenty-six minutes of physical activity a day for eight weeks significantly assisted in reducing ADHD symptoms in grade school students.

These researchers found out that regular physical activity programs can help young people by enhancing their brain function and their ability to perform mental tasks. Problems in the classroom may be resolved partly with more active time on the playground.

This knowledge is coming at a time when physical education classes and recess time are being severely reduced across the country. Since the passage of the No Child Left Behind Act in 2001, many schools have struggled to meet the academic standards being enforced. In order to find more time for academics, schools have cut out the time for active play. In 2007, the Robert Wood Johnson Foundation found that only 36 percent of students are getting the recommended amount of play. *The Journal of Physical Activity and Health* found that since the implementation of No Child Left Behind, schools have increased time devoted to reading by 47 percent and math by 37 percent. In return, there has been a 35 percent decrease in time for physical education and a 28 percent decrease in recess.

These changes may be impacting boys more than girls. According to the Centers for Disease Control and Prevention, 13.2 percent of boys were diagnosed with ADHD, compared with 5.6 percent of girls. Dr. Marjorie Montague said ADHD symptoms are different in boys than in girls. Boys with ADHD are more likely to be hyperactive and impulsive, while girls may be more likely to be inattentive, forgetful, easily distracted, or concentrate poorly.

Researchers are learning that exercise may be a key component in treating ADHD.

More Time to Party

Students also have been known to use Adderall as a "party drug." Because one of the results of using the drug is increased alertness, people think if they take the drug before a night of drinking, they will be able to party all night. By triggering the dopamine chemicals in the brain, a person is receiving the message that whatever is going on around him or her is important and deserves attention. This keeps the person alert and awake longer than if he or she was not taking the drug.

A third reason people abuse Adderall is because it decreases their appetite. Celebrities and others have been suspected of using Adderall to lose weight. Amphetamine, the primary ingredient in Adderall, speeds up a person's metabolism. However, weight loss from Adderall use tends to be temporary, and the weight will often return once a person stops taking the drug.

Too Much Too Soon

People who abuse the drug tend to take higher doses at once and through a different route. These dangerous methods allow them to achieve the desired effect quickly. A study in the *Journal of Clinical Psychiatry* found doses for intranasal, or snorting, have been reported as high as 200 milligrams. Those injecting the drug intravenously are reportedly taking doses ranging from 40 to 1,000 milligrams. These various methods of administration affect the length of time it takes for the drug's chemicals to reach the brain, which is when a person starts feeling the effects. When someone swallows

Mixing alcohol with Ritalin or Adderall is a recipe for disaster.

Safe Usage

The average prescribed dosage of Ritalin is one pill, two or three times a day, totaling 20 to 30 milligrams. The dosage is not to exceed 60 milligrams per day, even for adults. For Adderall, the recommended dose may begin with 5 milligrams in the morning and is not to exceed 30 milligrams per day. Doctors typically recommend their patients take medication thirty to forty-five minutes before a meal. Those prescribed Ritalin or Adderall are not supposed to take the drugs late in the day because doing so may make it difficult to sleep.

a pill, the drug must travel through most of the body and then be absorbed into the bloodstream. Once there, the chemicals rush to the brain. This process can take several minutes but will have a longer-lasting effect.

People who crush and then snort the pills experience the effects within minutes. Although the chemicals are absorbed into the bloodstream through the nasal passage, the effects are not as long lasting. Doses of Ritalin are supplied two ways: regular tablets and extended-release capsules. One extended-release capsule provides medication over a longer period of time. It reduces the need to take several regular tablets during the day. It does this by coating some of the drug with a material that takes time to dissolve in the body. The drug in the extended-release form is especially dangerous to snort because each capsule contains a higher dosage. Oftentimes the amount is above the lethal limit if taken all at once.

People who dissolve the pills in water and inject them directly into the bloodstream may feel the drug's effects within seconds. They also find the effects to wear off more quickly. Researchers have found that users who purposely seek the route of administration that gets the drug to the brain quickest are more likely to have problems with addiction.

CHAPTER THREE

Medications Don't Mix

IIT DOESN'T TAKE LONG FOR A PERSON to begin experiencing the negative effects of a drug he or she is abusing. The first effect is chemical. Ritalin and Adderall—whether taken legally or not—affect the dopamine levels in a person's brain. Dopamine at high levels is known to create a feeling of intense happiness and powerful energy that could make a person feel as if he or she could study or stay up all night and party. But there is a dangerous downside: when the effects of the drug have worn off, a person experiences a crash. This can be accompanied by feelings of being restless, jittery, depressed, and anxious. Users often find they have **cravings** for more of the drug, which they know will help

A person who becomes addicted to Adderall or Ritalin may find he or she has no energy when not on the drug. This leads them to a dangerous spiral where they get out of control.

the unpleasant feelings subside—but only for a while. And this is how people can become dependent on a drug.

First, users decide to experiment with the drug for a night of feeling high or extra focused. Then, they crash and discover how much they miss the "high and focused feeling" they just experienced. Physical dependence occurs when the body needs the drug to continue functioning normally.

Attempting to discontinue use of the drug can lead to **withdrawal**, which is a set of unpleasant symptoms that occur because the body has become so used to having the drug in its system. Withdrawal from Adderall can create depression, panic attacks, suicidal thoughts, foggy thinking, or sleep and appetite changes. It may also include an inability to focus, and anhedonia, which means an inability to experience pleasure or joy in activities that are normally pleasurable. Withdrawal from Ritalin may result in extreme fatigue, depression, or changes in the heart rhythm. People who find they have developed a dependence on the drug would be encouraged to **detox** under the care of a doctor or in a drug rehabilitation center. This would allow a person to wean his or her body off the drug at a healthier rate.

There are other potential dangers of long-term Ritalin use. Many drugs interact with Ritalin, increasing the risk of experiencing adverse side effects. A study in the *European Journal of Neuroscience* found that when Ritalin and certain antidepressants called Selective Serotonin Reuptake Inhibitors, or SSRIs, were taken together, there was an increased likelihood of addiction to the Ritalin. Ritalin taken with a

different type of antidepressant, called Monoamine Oxidase Inhibitors or MAOIs, can lead to a severe increase in blood pressure that may cause a stroke.

Additionally, Ritalin mixed with over-the-counter medicine taken for a cold that contains decongestants may lead to increased blood pressure or irregular heart rhythms. This shows that even these typically safe medicines may not be safe when mixed with other drugs. Those taking this drug under a doctor's care may be appropriately warned of these risks. Those buying it illegally or stealing it, however, are putting themselves—and their bodies—in extreme jeopardy.

Running the Stop Sign

As you have read, interactions between medications can be harmful. In fact, drugs grow more dangerous when other drugs are added to the mix. You have already read that Adderall is considered a party drug. If alcohol is involved, mixing it with Adderall may have devastating effects. You may have heard of people "passing out" or suddenly falling asleep when they drink unhealthy amounts of alcohol. This is the body's warning to stop drinking, and doing so may prevent alcohol poisoning. But a person using a stimulant such as Adderall to stay awake may never get the message. He or she could experience an alcohol overdose.

Ritalin taken with alcohol can produce side effects including drowsiness, anxiety, depression, or seizures. A study by the Substance Abuse and Mental Health Services Administration found that from 2005 to 2010, there was a three-fold increase in the amount of emergency room visits related to ADHD stimulant medications, from 5,212 to 15,585. Nearly half of the hospital visits were a result of people mixing ADHD stimulants with other drugs or alcohol.

The long-term effects of chronic Adderall use are also severe. Users may experience severe rashes, insomnia, irritability, and personality changes. The longer the drug is in your system, the more it can change who you are. Long-term users may experience hallucinations or delusional thinking. These are the same symptoms experienced by people who have schizophrenia, which can be a disabling mental illness in which those afflicted can lose touch with reality.

How a person chooses to abuse the drugs can also have long-term effects. There are several routes of administration for Ritalin or Adderall: by mouth, by snorting, or by injecting a drug dissolved in water. A person who has snorted Adderall for an extended period may experience deterioration in their nasal and sinus cavities, and their lung tissue.

A single injection of Ritalin can prove deadly. The pill may appear to dissolve completely in the water, but the tablets also contain a "filler" material that is insoluble, or impossible to dissolve. These solid filler materials can block small blood vessels when they are injected into the blood stream. A blocked blood vessel can cause serious damage to the lungs and the eyes in the short-term. Over time, permanent damage may be wreaked on blood vessels leading to the heart and brain, which can lead to high blood pressure, heart attacks, strokes, or death. Less severe, but very real effects of injecting any drug

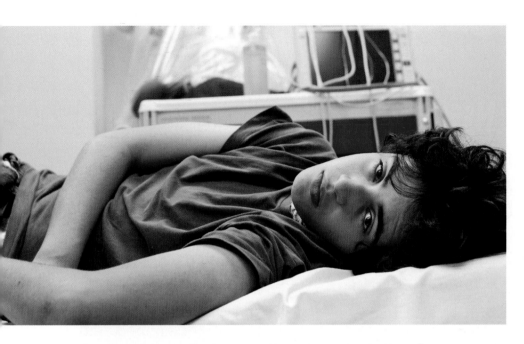

Injecting Ritalin can lead you quickly to the emergency room.

can be abscesses or blisters at the injection site. A person also may end up contracting communicable diseases such as HIV/AIDS or Hepatitis C by sharing a needle.

Gateway Drug

The Foundation for a Drug Free World also warns against many other short- and long-term effects of abusing stimulants. Short-term effects may include loss of appetite; increased heart rate; elevated blood pressure and body temperature; dilation, or widening, of pupils; disturbed sleep patterns; nausea; bizarre or violent behavior; hallucinations; irritability; panic or convulsions; and seizures. More common problems

THE NEED FOR SLEEP

The primary reason for stimulant abuse among teenagers is to increase alertness, attention, and focus; and to enhance performance in the classroom. For most students, however, a natural remedy already exists: getting more sleep!

Dr. James Maas, a Cornell professor of psychology and author of the book *Sleep for Success*, found that teenagers are getting an average of six hours of sleep per night instead of the recommended nine. Dr. Maas told a *New York Times* reporter that young people who don't sleep enough have a "cognitive ability worse than someone who is legally drunk."

The solution for someone worried about acing a test or finishing a paper on time does not include popping a pill. The answer for that person is to plan out his or her week appropriately and recognize that time spent under the covers is just as important as time hitting the books.

The best way to increase attention and concentration? Make sure to get enough sleep.

over the long term include liver, kidney, and lung damage; malnutrition and weight loss; disorientation or being extremely confused; drug dependence; depression; and brain damage.

It's clear the short- and long-term impact of abusing prescription drugs can be severe. However, for many, the story of drug abuse does not end with prescription drugs. The late Dr. Nadine Lambert, who was the director of the school

psychology program at the University of California at Berkeley, examined the relationship between Ritalin use and tobacco use. Her findings were that half of the youths who had been treated with Ritalin had become regular cigarette smokers by age seventeen, compared with 30 percent of teens who had never taken Ritalin.

Additionally, users of Ritalin and similar drugs fall into the highest percentage

Ritalin and Adderall could become gateway drugs, leading someone to experiment with other illegal substances.

of cocaine users. Dr. Lambert discovered that only 2 percent of the youths she studied who had never smoked cigarettes or had never taken Ritalin were dependent on cocaine as adults, while 40 percent of those who both smoked and were treated with stimulants such as Ritalin or Adderall had an addiction to cocaine as adults. We return to the mechanisms of the brain to understand this one. As a person uses or abuses a drug over time, he or she develops a **tolerance**. This means that the same amount of the drug doesn't have as much of an effect as it once did.

Two routes are available to a user when the drug isn't giving them the same high or focused feeling as it used to: the person can increase the dose or find a different drug. Cocaine, also a stimulant, may replicate some of the feelings experienced by individuals used to Ritalin or Adderall. Cocaine and Ritalin have similar chemical structures and act on the brain in similar ways, increasing the dopamine levels. For this reason, young people who have abused Ritalin or Adderall may be more likely to abuse cocaine in the long run.

CHAPTER FOUR

Change in Behavior

ACTRESS LINDSAY LOHAN IS FAMOUS FOR many things—not all of them good. She has endured two DUIs, a trip to jail, seven car accidents, six arrests, and six trips to rehab. The last trip to rehab lasted ninety days, and it was court-ordered. After the former Disney girl was released from rehab in the summer of 2014, she was interviewed by Oprah Winfrey.

During that interview, Lohan admitted that she was addicted to alcohol, had tried cocaine "ten to fifteen times," and that she had used Adderall regularly. People in the entertainment industry are abusing, and becoming addicted to, stimulants such as Adderall to stay thin. But Lohan said that's not the reason she was on the drug. She had been

Actress Lindsay Lohan, in tears during a court appearance, has fought a long battle with drug abuse, which she says began with Adderall.

diagnosed with ADHD as a teenager and had a prescription for it. She claims the drug calmed her down, and reportedly resumed her use of the drug after it had been taken away from her at a rehab clinic.

Doctors at the clinic in Los Angeles where Lohan had stayed told an entertainment website that they believed the actress was misdiagnosed with ADHD and that the Adderall may be the reason for her very erratic behavior. Lohan said that she had tried cocaine only "because it allowed me to drink more." This is also a side effect of Adderall, and Lohan's problems stemmed from long nights of partying.

She told Winfrey that after her extended rehab, she was both alcohol and Adderall free. This is fortunate for her, because she had clearly exhibited all the negative behaviors of people addicted to Adderall. How did the use of prescription stimulants get so out of control?

Despite the dangers and addictive properties of these drugs, many people don't think these stimulants can harm them because doctors prescribe them. Dr. Alan D. DeSantis, a professor of communications at the University of Kentucky, undertook a study to identify what students think about illegal prescription drug use. The results were that students find illegal prescription drug use "physically harmless and morally acceptable." Only 2 percent of students consider prescription drugs "very dangerous" while 81 percent feel that nonmedical use is "not dangerous at all" or only "slightly dangerous."

Drug Takes Over

Adderall or Ritalin can cause more than just physical problems. The drug can also impact a child's personality. Andrew K. Smith, author of *The Adderall Empire: A Life with ADHD and the Millennials' Drug of Choice*, described the impact the drug had on him. He wrote: "I had surrendered myself to Adderall and it was eating away at my soul. Adderall had created a false perception of who I was."

In addition to all the ways these drugs can harm a person's body, they can also change the chemistry in a person's brain, making them someone he or she does not even recognize.

Drug abuse can lead to long-term emotional effects.

Smith also claims that his generation has become more prone to taking the easy way out. "What has happened to my Adderall generation?" Smith wrote. "We can no longer have a rational thought. Have people lost their souls when they take this drug? The phrase 'Oh, I can't focus,' is sad. Not only is it sad, it's false. People can focus if they try hard enough, but they just give up and choose not to, begging for a drug to help them." While there is scientific merit in treating ADHD with Ritalin or Adderall, Smith suggests that we should consider looking for a longer-term and safer approach to treating the disorder instead of looking for that quick fix.

Out of Focus

Todd Essig, a clinical psychologist in New York City, warns against three stifling effects regular Adderall users can have. First, he warns a person's creativity may be undermined. He states that Adderall may assist a person in becoming a "more efficient solver of familiar problems." But the drug can also block creative thinking, the ability to find new solutions, or discover new problem-solving methods.

Essig also warns that a person's ego could be damaged. People develop self-confidence by knowing they have achieved a goal or have been successful. But if they use a drug to get that extra focus, they may not consider achievements as their own but as a product of the drug use. If someone thinks, "I couldn't have done it without the drug," they are not showing confidence in their abilities.

LEARN THE RISKS

Drug abuse prevention programs often overlook prescription drug abuse. A 2006 study found the Drug Abuse Resistance Education (D.A.R.E.) program—the most widespread drug prevention program in the country—to be among them. The study showed that "students, teachers, and school administrators who rely solely on the D.A.R.E. program for drug information may be underinformed about the potential dangers of prescription drug abuse." How could adults everywhere let this drug class slip through the cracks?

Unfortunately, many parents have been uneducated about Adderall and Ritalin use. Approximately 29 percent of parents surveyed by the Partnership at for Drug-Free Kids and the MetLife Foundation felt that Adderall was useful to improve a child's academic performance, even if they did not have a medical need for the drug. Only 14 percent of teens who talked with their parents about drugs had learned about the dangers of prescription drug abuse.

Sadly, people have been slow to realize the risks associated with prescription drug abuse. Anyone using any drug should get educated about its dangers and side effects.

Finally, recent reports have shown people are more productive if their mind takes a break or they take a nap from time to time. Getting one's body to rest while on a stimulant such as Adderall or Ritalin can be incredibly difficult. This is because the drug is robbing him or her of the chance to relax. This action can prevent a person from performing his or her best in school or at work.

If one person among a group of friends abuses drugs, it can harm his or her friends in a negative way. Brian Kelly, a professor at Purdue University and director of the school's Center for Research on Young People's Health, studies

Peer pressure or a desire to fit in leads many teens into illegal drug use.

drug use and youth cultures. He found that merely being associated with someone who uses drugs illegally could have an impact on those in his or her close peer group. Kelly's study shows that it's more than peer pressure that leads to experimentation.

"We find that friends are not actively pressuring them, but it's a desire to have a good time alongside friends that matters," Kelly said. "If there are high perceived social benefits or low perceived social consequences within the peer network, they are more likely to lead to a greater frequency of misuse, as well as a greater use of non-oral methods of administration and a greater likelihood of displaying symptoms of dependence."

What Kelly is saying is that if your friends are using drugs, you're more likely to use them, too. And there's also a greater chance that you will experiment with sniffing, smoking, or injecting drugs and begin to show signs of drug dependency or addiction.

Grades Affected

Many students use stimulants to help them get better grades, but the opposite may happen. The National Youth Risk Behavior Survey of 2009 investigated the connection between alcohol and drug use and the grades earned by students. For students who reported using a prescription drug without a doctor's prescription (this also includes drugs other than Ritalin and Adderall), 13 percent reported earning mostly As, 19 percent Bs, 26 percent Cs, and 41 percent reported earning mostly Ds and Fs. This shows a **correlation** between illegal drug use and poor school performance.

Outside the classroom, young people who use or abuse Ritalin may also face problems. The results of a recent experiment to determine the influence of Ritalin on the social behavior of rats were published in the scientific journal *Neuropsychopharmacology*. The study found that rats given Ritalin were less likely to "play" or be sociable with other rats. The researchers concluded that Ritalin

Abusing prescription drugs may lead to failure in the classroom.

appeared to be a "powerful blocker of normal, social play behavior." The purpose of Ritalin—for those prescribed the drug—is to inhibit erratic or unrestricted behaviors. This may also include a person's ability to freely interact with others.

Researchers for the scientific journal *Experimental and Clinical Psychopharmacology* examined the amount of a dose of Ritalin and how it changes social behavior. This study found that adolescents prescribed the drug might have improved social behavior with low doses. However, there appear to be "diminishing positive effects and an increased risk of negative effects with successively higher doses." This helps us understand that those prescribed the drug may experience behavioral benefits as long as it's in appropriately low doses. Those who do not need the drug are most likely to only experience social deficits.

The cost could also become a problem as a person slips more into drug dependency or addiction. One pill has been estimated to cost anywhere from $5 to $20 when purchased illegally. As a user's tolerance grows, they would need more

Using someone else's prescription drug is illegal. Doing so could cause you to be arrested.

pills to maintain the same effects. So what started as a $5 expense for one study session or one party with your friends could evolve into a habit costing hundreds of dollars a week.

The legal ramifications of possessing or distributing Ritalin could be even more costly. Under the Controlled Substances Act, an adult possessing Ritalin without a prescription may be punishable by a $1,000 fine, up to one year of jail time, or both. Getting caught a second time could lead to a $2,500 fine and two years in jail. And a third time could net a $5,000 fine and three years in prison. Selling or distributing the drug brings the punishment to another level: up to twenty years in prison and fines up to $1 million. A person who sells the drug to a user who dies or suffers significant bodily harm as a result can face at least twenty years in prison. Court systems have proven to be more lenient on teenagers who have been charged, but punishments vary from case to case and could still include fines, probation, and time spent in a juvenile detention center or a drug treatment program.

CHAPTER FIVE

A Job for a Pro

SEVERAL YOUNG PEOPLE, WHO DID NOT understand the risks of abusing Ritalin or Adderall, tried one of the drugs and found themselves hooked. They couldn't imagine going through a day without a couple of pills to help keep them focused and alert. Without the pills they felt **lethargic**, depressed, and didn't want to get out of bed at all. Without a daily dose, they may feel sick, have trouble concentrating, have severe mood swings, experience paranoia or anxiety, gain weight, or feel suicidal. To avoid all of these terrible feelings, they continued taking the drug. The cycle of addiction continues. They soon realize that their drug use has become a problem. What do they do now?

Teenagers who think they may have a problem with Ritalin or Adderall should talk to an adult they trust.

Depending on the individual factors involved—such as how long they have been abusing the drug, the amount of the drug they have taken, how often they were taking it and their body's physiology—they may respond in a variety of ways as they try to stop taking Ritalin or Adderall on a regular basis. There is one first step that everyone should take as they recognize that they want to move toward a drug-free life: tell an adult they trust that they need help.

Recover Slowly

What happens next is a decision for a medical professional. Depending on the dosage levels, a person may be encouraged to **taper** off the drug instead of quitting **cold turkey**—or stopping immediately. As you have read, a person's body can grow addicted to the drug, meaning he or she needs the drug to function "normally." It may be dangerous for that person to quit taking the drug altogether, and safer to gradually cut down on the amounts while being monitored by medical professionals. Again, this is a decision for a doctor to help a person make. What may follow, depending on the scope of the problem, could be an inpatient stay in a rehabilitation facility or outpatient treatment clinic. Outpatient treatment allows a person to still live at home but visit with a counselor or therapist during the week on one or more occasions, as prescribed.

Much needs to be done after a body recovers from the physical symptoms of addiction and potential withdrawal. Treatment for each individual will somewhat depend on the

52

reasons for the initial abuse. Ritalin and Adderall have fast become "study" drugs. If a student had grown used to popping a few pills before a big exam or pulling an all-nighter to write a big paper, his or her treatment may focus on how to more effectively use time or on how to create more outlined study plans to assure that an all-nighter isn't necessary. If a student once relied on the drug to ensure that all assigned schoolwork was completed, he or she would stick to a new schedule to finish all homework.

Treat the Problem

It is also possible that a person was using a stimulant to **self-medicate** an underlying illness. Oftentimes, people have illnesses for which they have not yet sought treatment. A common one is depression. A person with depression may find he or she:

- Feels depressed or is in an irritable mood for most of the day, nearly every day;
- has a decreased interest in, or receives no pleasure from, activities once thought to be enjoyable;
- undergoes significant changes in weight or appetite;
- changes sleep patterns and feels fatigue or loss of energy;
- feels worthless; and
- has a diminished ability to concentrate or has thoughts of suicide.

Untreated, depression can be miserable. Young people may find they feel better if they use a stimulant drug such as Adderall or Ritalin to make their moods higher and increase their alertness. But these drugs are not the answer—they are masking the symptoms of depression while potentially creating an additional problem: drug abuse or addiction. In some cases, it may be appropriate for a person who has abused Adderall or Ritalin to see a psychiatrist. A professional can determine if there is a need for appropriate medication to address underlying issues.

Some young people use a stimulant as a party drug, allowing them to stay up with their friends. However, once a person has recognized his or her drug use as a problem, he or she may be better off avoiding parties where others are abusing the drug. This could help prevent them being drawn back into drug use. They could try to find parties where this behavior is not prevalent or avoid parties altogether while developing a more appropriate plan for hanging out with friends.

A safe, socially positive option for teens involved in recovering from drug use is to attend Narcotics Anonymous meetings. It's important to remain socially active even if you're not using drugs, and Teen Narcotics Anonymous meetings may be a great place to meet new friends who are also committed to living a drug-free lifestyle. A study conducted by Dr. John F. Kelly, a researcher at Harvard Medical School, found teens who attended Narcotics Anonymous meetings were more likely to remain abstinent than teens recovering

There are plenty of ways to have fun that don't involve using drugs.

from drug use who did not attend meetings. "Given the need for social affiliation and peer-group acceptance outside of the family at this stage of life, peers can exert strong influence on the behavior of young people," Kelly explained.

How to Help

A person who hasn't been using these drugs might notice that a friend has gone too far with "experimenting" or "just having fun." The next step should be to tell that friend's parents, a teacher, or his or her own parents, to show concern for that friend and help him or her get the needed treatment. Talking with the friend directly and expressing worries can also be helpful.

It's also important to know that there may be a process to a friend accepting his or her drug use as a problem. This is referred to as the Stages of Change. The first stage is Precontemplation, meaning the person denies his or her

WARNING SIGNS OF RITALIN OR ADDERALL ABUSE

If a person suspects a friend is abusing Ritalin or Adderall, close attention should be paid to that friend's overall behavior.

Someone who is abusing the drug may complain about:
- Difficulty sleeping
- Unexplained stomach problems (could include diarrhea or constipation)
- Losing weight without exercising or dieting
- Lack of appetite
- Dizziness
- Blisters or skin abscesses (indicating needle use)
- Mood swings
- Headaches
- Rapid heart rate
- High blood pressure
- Nervousness or Restlessness
- Weaknesses in arms or legs

Knowing the signs of drug abuse may help you save a friend's life.

You may notice these changes in an abuser's behavior:
- Very alert and stimulated or lethargic and depressed
- Increased aggression
- Becomes irritable more easily than usual
- Expresses delusional thinking; being concerned that he or she is being followed or that people are out to get him or her
- Hallucinating: seeing, hearing, or feeling things that do not exist
- Stealing pills or money to buy pills
- Marked differences in commitment to schoolwork (could be a sudden disinterest or sudden improvement, due to staying up late to study)

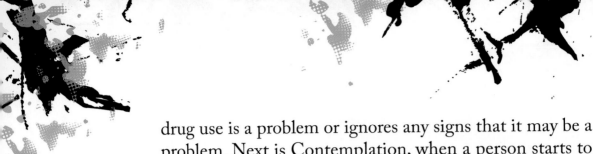

drug use is a problem or ignores any signs that it may be a problem. Next is Contemplation, when a person starts to recognize some problems caused by his or her drug use but has some conflicted emotions about changing his or her behaviors. Then comes Preparation, which includes small changes or collecting information about how to make changes, such as doing some research online about drug treatment or considering which adult to trust. Last is the Action stage, when a person is actively working toward achieving his or her goal of cutting back or eliminating drug use.

It is important to recognize that a friend may not yet be open to advice or feedback and may respond negatively to someone pointing out his or her drug use as a potential problem. This does not mean it is wrong to express concern. Voicing care for a friend may help him or her recognize that his or her behaviors are hurting those who care and that it may be time to consider change.

Glossary

abstinent The state of not using a drug.

addiction The state of being enslaved to a practice that is psychologically or physically habit-forming.

amphetamines A type of drug that stimulates the central nervous system. Adderall contains an amphetamine.

Attention Deficit Hyperactivity Disorder A neurodevelopmental disorder that leads to impairment in attention, hyperactivity, or impulsive behavior.

cold turkey To quit a habit abruptly and completely.

correlation A mutual connection between two or more things.

cravings Great or consistent desires for food, drink, or drugs.

depression A mood disorder that causes a persistent feeling of sadness.

detox To overcome drug dependence, usually under medical supervision.

dopamine A chemical in the brain that helps regulate emotion and movement.

dose A measured quantity of medicine prescribed to be taken at one time.

hallucinations Sensations of seeing, hearing, or feeling something that does not exist outside the mind.

lethargic The feeling of being drowsy or sluggish.

methylphenidate A type of drug that stimulates the central nervous system. Ritalin contains this drug.

neuron A functional cell in the central nervous system.

paradoxical Seemingly absurd or self-contradictory.

paranoia Irrational suspicion about, or the distrust of, others.

routes of administration Methods of taking or using a drug.

self-medicate To take drugs that are not prescribed to lessen feelings or symptoms.

stimulant A drug, food, or beverage that quickens or excites the senses.

taper To gradually stop using a drug.

tolerance A reduced reaction to regular doses of a drug, leading to a need for higher doses to achieve the same effects.

withdrawal Symptoms that start when the use of an addictive drug ends quickly, many of which may be unpleasant.

Find Out More

Books

Basia, Leonard, and Jeremy Roberts. *The Truth About Prescription Drugs.* Drugs and Consequences. New York: Rosen Publishing Group, 2011.

Kuhar, Michael J. *Substance Abuse, Addiction, and Treatment.* New York: Cavendish Square Publishing, 2012.

Porterfield, Jason. *Ritalin: A Difficult Choice.* Drug Abuse and Society. New York: Rosen Publishing Group, 2012.

Smith, Andrew K. *The Adderall Empire: A Life with ADHD and the Millennials' Drug of Choice.* New York: Morgan James Publishing, 2014.

Websites

KidsHealth
kidshealth.org

Uncover more facts about the health of kids and teens, watch videos, and test yourself with the site's Q&A.

National Institute of Mental Health

www.nimh.nih.gov/health/topics/attention-deficit
-hyperactivity-disorder-adhd/index.shtml

Learn more about Attention Deficit Hyperactivity Disorder, its signs and symptoms, who is at risk, and treatments.

NIDA for Teens

teens.drugabuse.gov

Created for middle and high school students and their teachers, the National Institute for Drug Abuse website provides accurate and timely information for use in and out of the classroom. Discover the science behind drug abuse and the facts teens should know before putting any substance into their bodies.

Partnership for Drug-Free Kids

www.drugfree.org

By exploring this website, families can find the information they need to understand the everchanging drug landscape, which now includes abuse of prescription drugs and over-the-counter cough medicine.

Index

Page numbers in **boldface** are illustrations. Entries in **boldface** are glossary terms.

About the Author

Jackie F. Stanmyre is a former award-winning journalist at the *Star-Ledger* of Newark, NJ. She currently works as a mental health and addiction counselor. She lives in Montclair, NJ, with her husband and their two cats.